W9-CTS-984

KING
OF THE
DINOSAURS

by
Dennis Schatz

Walking T. Rex Skeleton
Copyright © 2005 becker&mayer!
Published by Tangerine Press, an imprint of Scholastic Inc.
557 Broadway, New York, NY 10012
All rights reserved.

Scholastic and Tangerine Press and associated logos are trademarks of Scholastic Inc.

No part of this book may be reproduced, stored in a retrieval system, or transmitted
in any form or by any means, electronic, mechanical, photocopying, recording, or
otherwise, without the prior permission of Tangerine Press.

Produced by becker&mayer!, Ltd.
11010 Northup Way
Bellevue, WA 98004
www.beckermayer.com
If you have questions or comments about this product, send e-mail to
infobm@beckermayer.com

Written by Dennis Schatz
Art direction and design by Karrie Lee
Edited by Betsy Henry Pringle
Toy development by Todd Rider
Production management by Katie Stephens

Illustration credits:
Experiment illustrations by Karrie Lee
Assembly illustrations by Ryan Hobson
Pages 3–7: Christopher Johnson.
Pages 8–9: Davide Bonadonna.
Pages 10–11: T. rex skull, tooth, and T. rex running by Christian Kitzmüller; T. rex
stomach by Davide Bonadonna.
Pages 12–13: Lungs by Davide Bonadonna; nasal bone by Christian Kitzmüller; T. rex
and Triceratops by Christopher Johnson.
Pages 14–15: Coprolite and bird heart by Davide Bonadonna; nest of eggs by
Christian Kitzmüller.
Pages 16–17: Archaeopteryx by David Bonadonna; fossil by Christian Kitzmüller;
warm-blooded animals by Christopher Johnson; cold-blooded animals by
Bob Greisen.
Pages 18–19: Asteroid by Christian Kitzmüller; volcano by Christopher Johnson.
Pages 20–21: T. rexes by David Bonadonna; Parasaurolophus by Christopher
Johnson; dinosaur arms by Christian Kitzmüller.
Pages 22–23: Christopher Johnson.
Pages 24–25: Photo of Jack Horner © Museum of the Rockies; photo of Sue at the
Field Museum © Paul Townend.

All rights reserved.
Printed, manufactured, and assembled in China
10 9 8 7 6 5 4 3 2 1
ISBN: 0-439-77757-7
04447

Walking with T. Rex

TYRANNOSAURUS REX—BETTER known as T. rex—was one of the largest meat eaters to ever walk the earth. This particular king of the dinosaurs lived by a river in what is today Montana. As he walks along the riverbank, he hears the roar of an injured Triceratops (try-SARE-uh-tops). Could this sound be coming from the animal that will be his next meal?

His four-foot-long head swivels in the direction of the noise. His bulging eyes rotate forward. This gives him the sharp vision he needs to find the source of the noise. His sensitive nose can detect the scent of blood twenty miles away. He smells the blood seeping from the wounded Triceratops. He makes his way toward the noise and smell.

The T. rex stomps forward, his knees higher than your head. His massive feet sink several inches into the muddy bank. With each step, he produces a loud sucking sound and leaves deep footprints.

This was the life of T. rex 70 million years ago. But with no humans to record these events, how do we know this happened? Turn the page to discover what we know about these giant animals that lived millions of years ago—and how we know it.

Finding T. Rex

FOSSILS FROM DINOSAURS buried in the ground tell us what life was like 70 million years ago. To see how fossils form, let's continue to watch T. rex as he searches for food.

T. rex gets buried

The T. rex finds the source of the noise. Three human-sized Dromaeosauruses (DRO-mee-o-SAWR-us-uz) surround a Triceratops they just killed. The T. rex is patient. He lets the Dromaeosauruses get their fill of Triceratops meat. Once they leave, he gets to feast on leftovers. He rips off a large chunk of meat with his six-inch-long teeth. He swallows the bite whole. As the T. rex is about to take a second bite, a flashflood that was produced by a thunderstorm earlier in the day rounds a bend in the river.

All of a sudden, the T. rex is tumbling around underwater. He can't breathe and quickly drowns. When the water settles down, the body is buried among the mud, rocks, and bushes left behind. In a few months, the flesh and the soft parts of the T. rex rot away. Over millions of years, more floods bury the bones deeper in mud. Pressure from the overlying rock and dirt slowly turns the mud to rock. Water, carrying dissolved minerals, seeps into the rocks. These minerals fill the small air spaces in the bones, turning the bones into fossils.

Discovering T. rex's bones

Most of the time, fossils remain hidden deep underground. But not this time. A construction crew building a new road accidentally discovers the T. rex fossils.

If you were a *paleontologist* (PAY-lee-un-TALL-uh-jist), a scientist who studies fossils, this would be your workplace. You use bulldozers and jackhammers to break away rock and expose the T. rex fossils. It is 100 degrees in the shade, but there is no shade. The equipment kicks up clouds of dirt that mix with the sweat streaming down your face. You look and feel grimy.

Once you get near the fossils, your work needs a more delicate touch. You begin using handheld tools—pickaxes, shovels, hammers, chisels, and brushes. These let you get near the fossils without damaging them. Fossils crack or break easily when exposed to the air. You quickly and carefully wrap them in wet paper towels. A covering of burlap soaked in plaster then protects the fossils, much like a cast protects a broken bone. Now the fossils are ready for transport back to your laboratory at the natural history museum.

What Good Are Bones?

AFTER YOU CLEAN the fossilized bones, your job is to reconstruct the dinosaur's skeleton and figure out what we can learn from T. rex's bones. You do this by looking at the skeletons of other dinosaurs and of animals alive today.

Bones give your body its shape

Look at your own body to see what you can learn about bones. Your bones are a framework structure that gives your body its shape and helps you stand up straight. They allow you to sit, run, and roll up into a ball to do a somersault. Without your bones, you would be nothing but a big, soft blob!

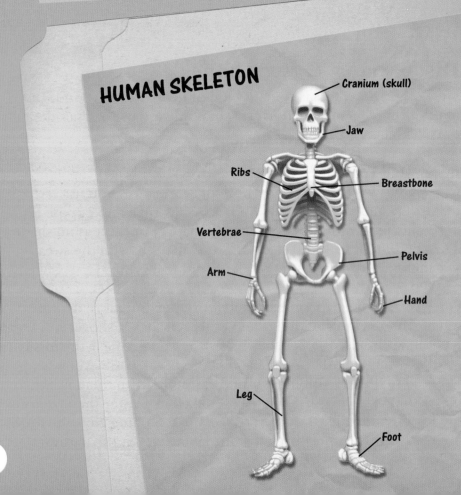

HUMAN SKELETON

- Cranium (skull)
- Jaw
- Ribs
- Breastbone
- Vertebrae
- Pelvis
- Arm
- Hand
- Leg
- Foot

Fossilized bones

Fossilized dinosaur bones are much harder and heavier than plain bones. This is because all the spaces in the bones, including the spaces that carried blood vessels, filled with minerals over the millions of years the bones were buried.

Compare your skeleton to T. rex's

Look at the bones in a human skeleton. Compare the bones to the skeleton of T. rex. Which bones look similar and which look very different? Why do you think that is? Turn the page to discover what paleontologists learned by studying the fossilized bones of T. rex.

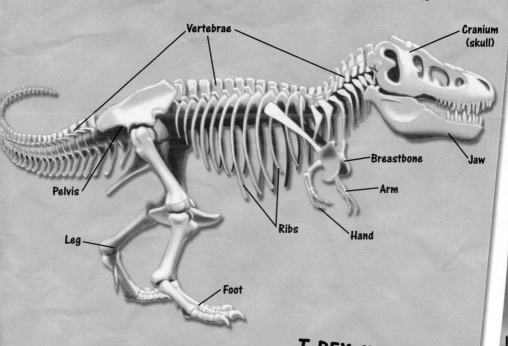

Vertebrae

Cranium (skull)

Breastbone

Jaw

Arm

Pelvis

Ribs

Hand

Leg

Foot

T. REX SKELETON

What T. Rex's Bones Tell Us

T REX FOSSILS are found in the western United States and Canada. Most of the time, only part of the skeleton is found. In 1990, an almost complete skeleton was discovered in South Dakota. This skeleton— named Sue—is now on display in the Field Museum in Chicago.

Here is what we know from looking at T. rex's skeleton:

T. rex grew to be as long as 40 feet—as long as a small school bus.

It had teeth that it used to bite into meat.

It walked upright on two massive back legs.

It had two front arms, but they were so short they could not reach its mouth.

It had a long tail, which was used to balance the weight of its upper body.

By looking at the size and thickness of the bones, scientists think T. rex weighed over five tons (10,000 pounds), more than the weight of a fully loaded small school bus.

How well did T. rex see?

T. rex's eye sockets allowed it to rotate its eyes so they pointed forward. It could then use its *parallax* (PARE-eh-lax) vision to judge the distance to its prey and to quickly maneuver around it. Your eyes also point forward, which is critical when you need to judge how far to kick a soccer ball or throw a football.

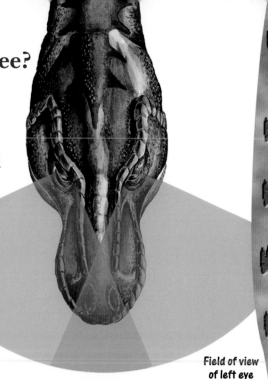

Field of view of right eye

Field of view overlap

Field of view of left eye

TRY THIS: Parallax vision works because each eye compares the position of something close to something far away. Hold your finger right in front of your eyes and wink your eyes so that you look at your finger with one eye and then other. Your finger will appear to jump back and forth compared to objects in the background.

Repeat this with your finger held far from your eye. The amount your finger appears to move against the background is less.

Your brain uses this information to help you determine the distance to an object.

HOLDING FINGER UP CLOSE TO YOUR FACE

HOLDING FINGER FAR AWAY FROM YOUR FACE

What T. Rex's Bones Tell Us

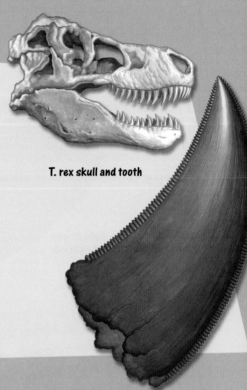

How did T. rex eat?

T. rex's six-inch-long teeth had ridges called *serrations* (sare-A-shuns). These look like the ridges on a steak knife. They punctured and split the meat of T. rex's prey. The massive muscles in T. rex's jaw then ripped out large chunks of meat, which often included chunks of bone.

T. rex skull and tooth

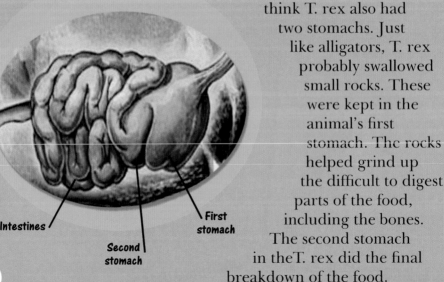

T. rex did not chew, but instead swallowed its food whole. Alligators eat the same way. Alligators have two stomachs. This makes many paleontologists think T. rex also had two stomachs. Just like alligators, T. rex probably swallowed small rocks. These were kept in the animal's first stomach. The rocks helped grind up the difficult to digest parts of the food, including the bones. The second stomach in theT. rex did the final breakdown of the food.

Intestines

Second stomach

First stomach

How did T. rex stand and run?

The location of T. rex's hips compared to the *vertebrae* (VERT-eh-bruh) on its back shows that T. rex moved with its back horizontal to the ground. Strong muscles helped keep the tail stretched out horizontally. The huge animal moved with its head far forward. Its tail moved quickly to counterbalance its head. The tail could also easily whip back and forth to protect it from any enemies.

TRY THIS: Animals that walk on two feet need to have their weight evenly distributed to the front and back of their feet. Otherwise, they will fall over.

Stand against a solid wall with your heels and hips flat against the wall. Have a friend put a coin a foot in front of your feet. Don't move your heels or hips away from the wall. Try to pick up the coin without bending your knees. You will fall over before you reach the coin!

T. rex would have fallen flat on its face if it had not had a long, massive tail to counterbalance its head, neck, and chest.

COUNTERBALANCE EXPERIMENT

How did T. rex breathe?

The rib bones in T. rex's upper body had openings for *air sacs* that attached to its lungs. This is similar to the way birds breathe. If T. rex had air sacs, it probably took two breaths to move air through its body. Here's how it worked. When T. rex first inhaled (sucked air in), air filled the air sacs. When it first exhaled (pushed air out), the air moved to the lungs instead of leaving the body. With its second inhale, the air in the lungs moved to more air sacs. With the second exhale, the air finally left the body. This "two-step breathing" system kept more air moving through T. rex's body.

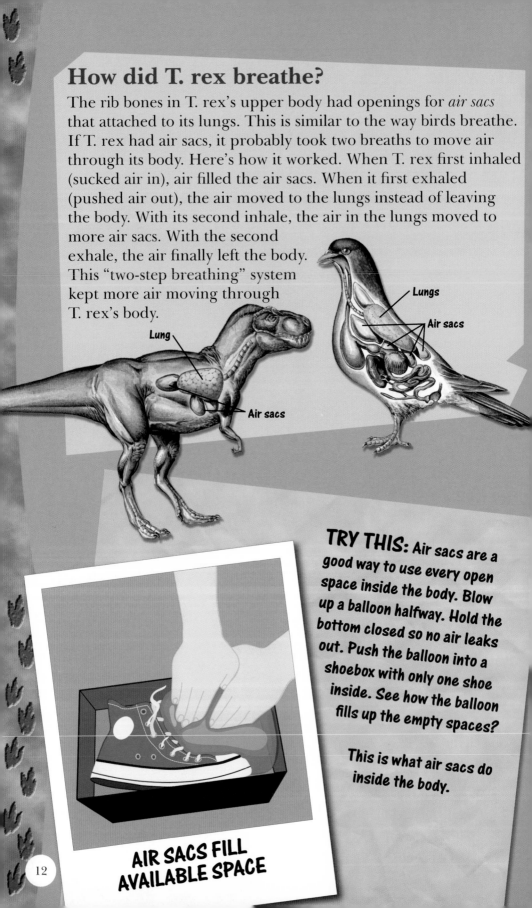

Lungs

Air sacs

Lung

Air sacs

TRY THIS: Air sacs are a good way to use every open space inside the body. Blow up a balloon halfway. Hold the bottom closed so no air leaks out. Push the balloon into a shoebox with only one shoe inside. See how the balloon fills up the empty spaces?

This is what air sacs do inside the body.

AIR SACS FILL AVAILABLE SPACE

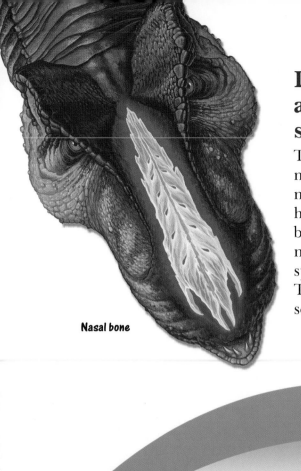

Nasal bone

Did T. rex have a keen sense of smell?

T. rex had a long, narrow nasal bone above a large nasal cavity. The bone had many small holes for blood vessels. The large nasal cavity provided space for many nerves. This gave T. rex a keen sense of smell.

Clues About T. Rex Aren't Just in the Bones

OTHER CLUES ABOUT the nature of T. rex are found in fossils that are not bones.

T. rex droppings?

Fossilized dinosaur "droppings" (coprolites) are a rare find. A coprolite found in Canada near a T. rex named Scotty is 21 inches long and weighs 15 pounds. It was full of ground-up bones. This proves T. rex had jaws and teeth strong enough to bite into bone and that it swallowed its food whole.

Coprolite

T. rex eggs?

No T. rex eggs have been found. But paleontologists have found fossilized eggs from at least 80 other kinds of dinosaurs. This makes scientists think that all dinosaurs laid eggs. Although some dinosaurs grew to be hundreds of feet long and weighed thousands of pounds, their eggs were probably no bigger than a large grapefruit. Big eggs require thick shells so they won't break. But thick shells don't allow oxygen and water through so the baby can breathe and grow. Plus, the shell must be thin enough for the baby to break it from the inside when it is ready to hatch.

Nest of eggs

14

T. rex footprints?

Imprints of dinosaur feet, showing where they walked in the mud, also exist. These imprints turn to rock if left undisturbed for millions of years. Only a few T. rex footprint tracks exist. We have learned little from them. If more tracks are found, scientists can tell how fast the dinosaur was moving when it made the tracks. The scientists do this by measuring the distance between each step and comparing that with the size of the animal's footprint.

Dinosaur trackway

T. rex heart?

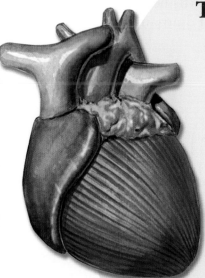

Bird's four-chambered heart

Usually the soft insides of the dinosaurs would rot away before they could become fossils. But a rare find in South Dakota revealed the fossilized heart of a plant-eating dinosaur. Paleontologists used a computer tomography (CT) scanner to look inside the heart. In this case, the paleontologists found that the dinosaur had a four-chambered heart like you and like birds.

Many Questions Remain

W E KNOW MUCH about T. rex and other dinosaurs. But there is still much that scientists are learning from new discoveries and new ways to study the fossils.

Did T. rex have feathers?

The skin and feathers of dinosaurs usually rot away before they become fossils. But scientists have found fossilized imprints of dinosaur skin and feathers that were made in mud.

In 1861 in Germany, paleontologists discovered the 145-million-year-old fossil of Archaeopteryx (ar-key-OP-te-rix). It has the bone structure of a dinosaur, but it had feathers. Since 1996, five different types of dinosaurs with feathers have been discovered. This adds more evidence for birds being the descendants of dinosaurs.

Archaeopteryx

Study of skin imprints may help scientists learn how many dinosaurs had feathers. One sample of T. rex skin imprints looks like the skin of a plucked chicken. Skin imprints from another large, meat-eating dinosaur show a bumpy, scaly hide similar to the skin on the legs of many birds. Even if the adult T. rex had no feathers, perhaps a baby T. rex had downy feathers.

Fossilized Archaeopteryx

Was T. rex cold-blooded or warm-blooded?

Warm-blooded animals keep their bodies at a constant temperature. Coverings of fur or feathers, layers of fat, and a generous flow of blood help them do this. Birds and mammals (such as humans, lions, and dogs) are all warm-blooded.

Examples of warm-blooded animals

Cold-blooded animals use sunlight to heat up their bodies. Or they move to the shade to cool off. Reptiles (such as snakes, lizards, and crocodiles) are cold-blooded. Cold-blooded animals usually eat less and are not as active as warm-blooded animals.

Cold-blooded animals grow more in warm weather than in cold weather, so their bones have *growth lines*. Growth lines are similar to the growth rings on trees.

Examples of cold-blooded animals

The bones of warm-blooded animals show many pathways for blood vessels, but no growth lines. Scientists look at T. rex bones under the microscope to determine whether dinosaurs were warm-blooded or cold-blooded. At this point, they are not sure, because they have found growth rings *and* blood vessels. Perhaps dinosaurs were a combination of both.

How Did the Dinosaurs Become Extinct?

Was it a comet or asteroid?

Most scientists believe that a comet or asteroid hit our planet 65 million years ago in what is now the Gulf of Mexico. It left a crater 80 miles across at the bottom of the water. This messenger of doom blasted rocks, dirt, and water into the air, creating a layer of ash that spread around the world and blocked the sunlight. The planet's temperature dropped. Many plants and animals could not survive. All the dinosaurs became extinct. And more than half of all animal types did not make it through the catastrophe.

Was it diseases?

Another possibility is that many animals made migrations from Asia to North America across a land bridge that existed between Siberia and Alaska. These migrating animals brought new diseases. Many of the animals already living in the area got sick and died.

Was it volcanoes?

Not everyone agrees that a comet or asteroid impact caused the extinction of the dinosaurs. Some scientists think that there was a period of unusually high volcanic activity around the world 65 million years ago. This could have filled the skies with ash that circled the globe and caused the changes in the weather that killed the dinosaurs.

A comet or asteroid is the most likely

Evidence in *sedimentary* (seh-deh-MEN-tar-y) rocks presents the best argument for why the dinosaurs' extinction was probably caused by a comet or asteroid. Sedimentary rocks are formed when layers of mud and dirt (sediment) are laid down on top of each other over millions of years. The pressure of all the layers turns the sediment into rocks.

Scientists look for sedimentary rock formations that have been created over time. The rock layer from 65 million years ago contains a high level of the rare element *iridium* (i-RID-ee-um). The level in this layer is higher than in any layer created before or after. These higher levels of iridium are only found in comets or asteroids. If an object from outer space hit the Earth, the resulting explosion would cause debris to fly high into the air. The iridium from the exploded comet or asteroid would mix with this debris as it circled the Earth. As the material settled to the ground, it would leave a layer of sediment rich in iridium.

What We Will Never Know from T. Rex's Bones

NEW DISCOVERIES AND more study may reveal new things about T. rex and the life of dinosaurs. But some things will probably never be known about T. rex and its dinosaur relatives.

What color was T. rex?

Animals often have skin colors that help them blend into their surroundings so they are not easily seen by other animals. Some mixture of green, brown, and gray would do this. Since T. rex was an ancestor of today's birds, maybe the males and females had different coloring like many of today's birds. Maybe the crest of the head had bright colors to attract a mate.

What kind of sound did T. rex make?

T. rex had holes in its skull for ears. So paleontologists think they made noises to communicate with other animals. But no one is sure what kind of sound T. rex made. However, much research has been done on the sound made by Parasaurolophus (PAR-ah-saw-ROL-oh-fus). It had a large crest with a 4 ½-foot-long nasal cavity.

Parasaurolophus nasal cavity

Scientists use computer models to determine what the sound would be. Their experiments revealed that the Parasaurolophus emitted a low rumbling sound when it blew air through the cavities in its crest.

What were T. rex's tiny arms used for?

T. rex's arms were so short they could not reach its mouth. What good were they if they didn't help put food in its mouth? The arms were even too short to help hold down prey while killing it.

T. rex's arms weren't strong enough to keep it from getting hurt in a fall. Imagine a T. rex running after its evening meal. The huge dinosaur trips and falls forward, throwing its arms out to break its fall. Scientists think the arms would shatter as the five-ton animal hit the ground.

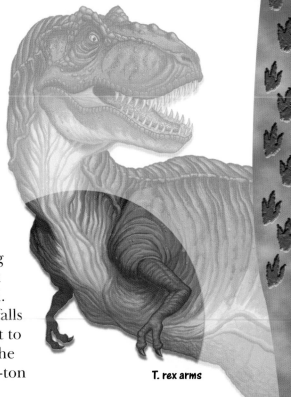

T. rex arms

Some scientists think T. rex used its arms to help it mate with another T. rex, but no modern-day animal has similar front arms for scientists to study.

Other meat-eating dinosaurs, like Allosaurus and Dromaeosaurus, had similar-looking arms. But their arms were long enough to help them eat food. Some scientists think that the arms slowly became useless parts of the body as the large meat-eating dinosaurs changed size and shape over thousands of years.

Allosaurus arms

Other Dinosaurs That Lived with T. Rex

O THER DINOSAURS LIVED in Montana 70 million years ago. Here is what we know about some of them by looking at their fossilized bones:

Dromaeosaurus (drom-ee-o-SAWR-us)
Meaning of name: Swift lizard
Weight: 50 pounds (22.7 kg.)
Length: 5–6 feet (1.5–1.8 m.)
It gave its name to the group of dinosaurs called dromaeosaurs—also known as "raptors." Raptors had large slicing-toes on each rear foot. The toe would swing back to be out of the way when running, but then make a broad sweeping motion to cut into the side of the animal's prey.

Ornithomimus (or-ni-thuh-MI-mus)
Meaning of name: Bird mimic
Weight: 300 pounds (136 kg.)
Length: 15 feet (4.6 m.)
Ornithomimus looked much like an ostrich! It probably used it toothless beak to eat worms, bugs, and seeds.

Pachycephalosaurus (pack-ee-SEFF-ah-low-SAWR-us)
Meaning of name: Thick-headed lizard
Weight: 1,000 pounds (453.6 kg.)
Length: 15 feet (4.6 m.)
It is best known for its enlarged head and thick skull. The skull may have been used for butting against other Pachycephalosauruses or was for show to attract a mate.

Dromaeosaurus

Triceratops

Ornithomimus   Pachycephalosaurus

Triceratops (try-SARE-uh-tops)

Meaning of name: Three-horned face
Weight: 10,000 to 16,000 pounds (4,536–7,257 kg.)
Length: 30 feet (9.1 m.)
It got its name from the two long horns (up to three feet long) above its eyes and the one short horn (about a foot long) above its nose. Scrapes that appear to be from the teeth of a T. rex make scientists think T. rex hunted Triceratops.

Parasaurolophus (PAR-ah-saw-ROL-oh-fus)

Meaning of name: Beside crested lizard
Weight: 6,000 pounds (2,722 kg.)
Length: 40 feet (12.2 m.)
This dinosaur had a mouth like a cow—a bony ridge ran across the top front of the mouth instead of teeth. This ridge clamped down on a flat plate on the bottom jaw. Parasaurolophus used this ridge to strip leaves from trees.

Edmontosaurus (ed-MON-toe-SAWR-us)

Meaning of name: Edmonton lizard
Weight: 8,000 pounds (3,629 kg.)
Length: 42 feet (12.8 m.)
The shape of its upper jaw suggests that it had skin flaps above its nose. These could be inflated to help attract a mate or to make loud honking sounds.

Edmontosaurus

Parasaurolophus

Growing Up to Be a Paleontologist

Do you want to find your own fossils? Here are a few things you need to know before you begin:

 Fossils are found in sedimentary rock where sand, mud, or silt covers the plant or animal. Some names of sedimentary rocks are shale, sandstone, limestone, and gypsum.

 The best place to look for fossils is where sedimentary rock has worn away, revealing the fossils. Good places to look for fossils are where roads are cut into the side of a hill or where water has eroded the land into ravines.

 Look for rocks that are a different shape and color than the surrounding rocks.

 If you suspect you have found a fossil, take it to your local rock club or natural history museum.

Before you go prospecting, be sure you have permission from the owner of the land to be there!

JACK HORNER AT EGG MOUNTAIN

If you love hunting fossils, then maybe you can grow up to be like John (Jack) Horner, one of the best-known paleontologists in the world. Horner discovered the fossilized remains of Maiasaura (good mother lizard) in 1978. This find included the first nest of baby dinosaurs. It showed that the adults cared for the babies after they were born. Jack Horner is lead paleontologist at the Museum of the Rockies at Montana State University in Bozeman, Montana.

Sue on display at the Field Museum.

Sue and Bob

Sue is the most complete T. rex skeleton discovered (so far). The dinosaur was named after Sue Hendrickson, who discovered the fossils partially sticking out of the ground on a ridge in South Dakota in 1990. In 2003, paleontologists excavated a T. rex they call "Bob" in northeastern Montana. Estimated to be 68 million years old, Bob is the oldest T. rex on record.

Now it's time to build
your own Walking
T. Rex Skeleton!

Assembly Instructions

Parts:

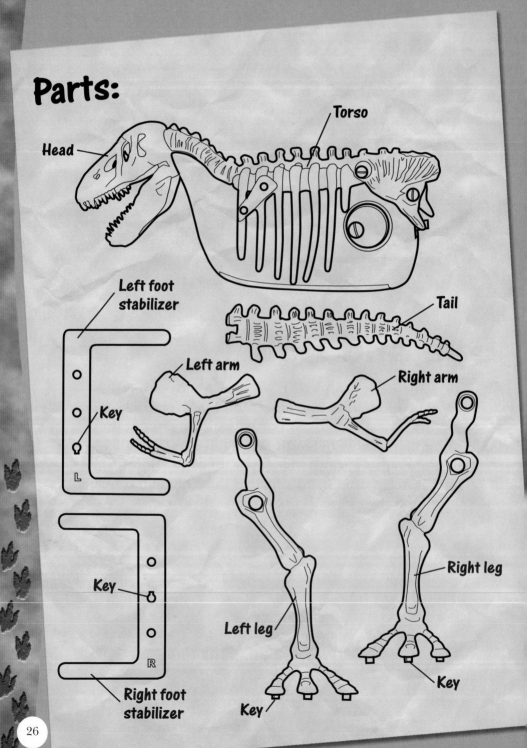

- Head
- Torso
- Left foot stabilizer
- Tail
- Key
- Left arm
- Right arm
- Key
- Right leg
- Key
- Left leg
- Right foot stabilizer
- Key

Walking on Two Legs

Walking on two legs is hard! The body's *center of gravity* shifts with every step. Your brain helps you adjust your balance so you don't fall over, but your Walking T. Rex Skeleton doesn't have a brain. It also doesn't have a long, muscular tail that moves back and forth as it walks. That's why your Walking T. Rex Skeleton needs those funny-looking feet.

TRY THIS: The center of gravity is the point at which the mass of an object is balanced. Try this experiment to see how a long tail helped T. rex balance. You will need a ruler and a lump of clay.

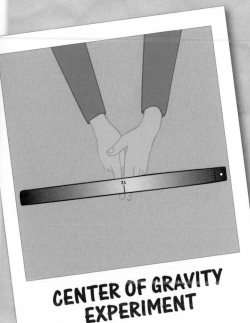

Support the ruler on the ends of two fingers. Slide your fingers together, adjusting them until the ruler is balanced when your two fingers are touching. Notice the measurement number where the balance point is. The place where your fingers meet and the ruler is balanced is the ruler's center of gravity.

CENTER OF GRAVITY EXPERIMENT

Now add a small lump of clay to one end of the ruler and try to balance the ruler on your two fingers again. What happened to the center of gravity? Think of the lump of clay as T. rex's big, heavy head.

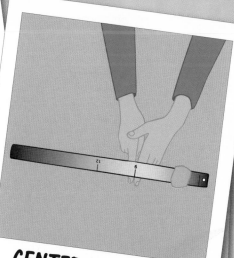

CENTER OF GRAVITY EXPERIMENT WITH CLAY

27

How to Assemble Your Walking T. Rex Skeleton

Attaching the Legs to the Torso

1. With the prongs pointing inward (see Figure 1), press the right foot stabilizer onto the right foot (the letter R will be at the back of the T. rex).

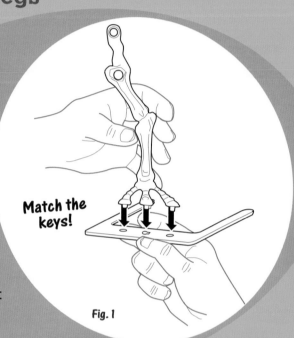

Match the keys!

Fig. 1

2. Holding the right leg in one hand (with the leg pointing down) and the torso in the other hand, press hole A over pin A and then position hole B over pin B (see Figure 2).

3. Gently press the right leg onto the torso until it clicks.

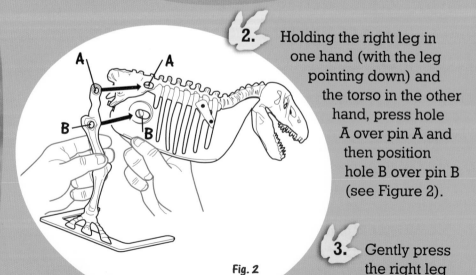

Fig. 2

4. With the prongs pointing inward (see Figure 3), press the left foot stabilizer onto the left foot (the letter L will be at the back of the T. rex).

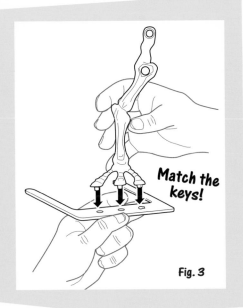

Match the keys!

Fig. 3

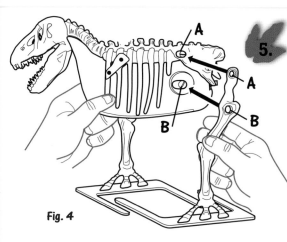

Fig. 4

5. Holding the left leg in one hand (with the leg pointing down) and the torso in the other hand, press hole A over pin A and then position hole B over pin B (see Figure 4).

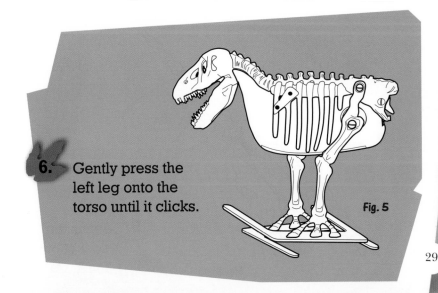

6. Gently press the left leg onto the torso until it clicks.

Fig. 5

Attaching the Arms and Tail to the Torso

7. Gently press the two right arm pins into the holes on the right side of the T. rex (see Figure 6).

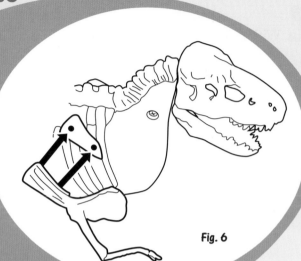

Fig. 6

8. Gently press the two left arm pins into the holes on the left side of the T. rex (see Figure 7).

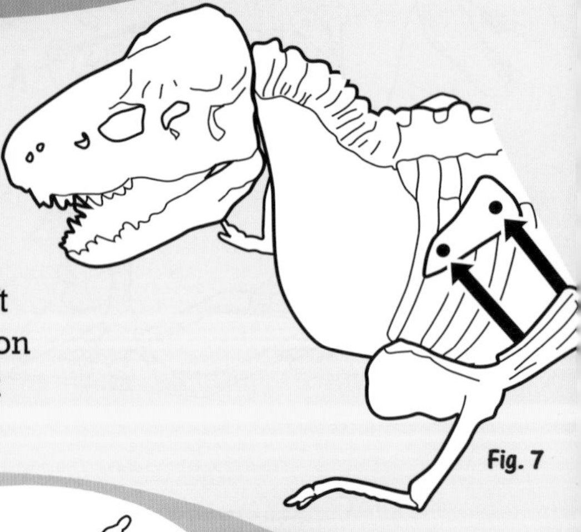

Fig. 7

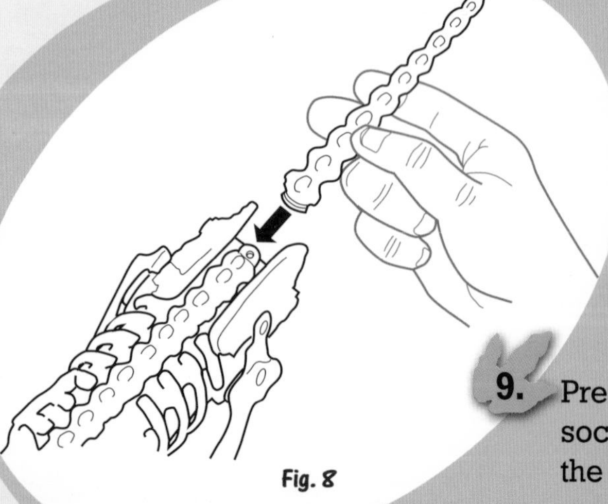

9. Press the tail onto the socket on the back of the T. rex (see Figure 8).

Fig. 8